Generational Family Tree

Creator: _____

Date: _____

Our Family history

_____

_____

_____

_____

_____

_____

_____

_____

_____

_____

_____

FAMILY HISTORY QUESTIONS TO ASK

Did you know your maternal grandparents? What do you remember about them most?

_____

_____

_____

Did you know you paternal grandparents? What do you most remember about them?

_____

_____

_____

Who's the oldest relative you can remember meeting?

_____

_____

_____

_____

Did you have a favorite relative? Who was the relative you most enjoyed seeing?

_____

_____

_____

_____

Who was the family historian in the family when you were growing up?

_____

_____

_____

_____

Remembering back to your childhood, was there a storyteller in your family?

_____

_____

_____

_____

Who was the funniest person among your relatives?

_____

_____

_____

Which relative do you wish you had known better and why?

_____

_____

_____

_____

What family traditions did you most enjoy?

_____

_____

_____

What haven't I asked that you'd like to tell me about?

_____

_____

_____

Name	Date of Birth	Location of Birth	Date of Marriage	Location of Marriage	Date of Death	Location of Death

NOTES

_____

_____

_____

Name	Date of Birth	Location of Birth	Date of Marriage	Location of Marriage	Date of Death	Location of Death

NOTES

Name	Date of Birth	Location of Birth	Date of Marriage	Location of Marriage	Date of Death	Location of Death

NOTES

Name	Date of Birth	Location of Birth	Date of Marriage	Location of Marriage	Date of Death	Location of Death

NOTES

Name	Date of Birth	Location of Birth	Date of Marriage	Location of Marriage	Date of Death	Location of Death

NOTES

Name	Date of Birth	Location of Birth	Date of Marriage	Location of Marriage	Date of Death	Location of Death

NOTES

Name	Date of Birth	Location of Birth	Date of Marriage	Location of Marriage	Date of Death	Location of Death

NOTES

_____

_____

_____

_____

Name	Date of Birth	Location of Birth	Date of Marriage	Location of Marriage	Date of Death	Location of Death

NOTES

Name	Date of Birth	Location of Birth	Date of Marriage	Location of Marriage	Date of Death	Location of Death

NOTES

Name	Date of Birth	Location of Birth	Date of Marriage	Location of Marriage	Date of Death	Location of Death

NOTES

Name	Date of Birth	Location of Birth	Date of Marriage	Location of Marriage	Date of Death	Location of Death

NOTES

Name	Date of Birth	Location of Birth	Date of Marriage	Location of Marriage	Date of Death	Location of Death

NOTES

Name	Date of Birth	Location of Birth	Date of Marriage	Location of Marriage	Date of Death	Location of Death

NOTES

_____

_____

_____

Name	Date of Birth	Location of Birth	Date of Marriage	Location of Marriage	Date of Death	Location of Death

NOTES

Name	Date of Birth	Location of Birth	Date of Marriage	Location of Marriage	Date of Death	Location of Death

NOTES

Name	Date of Birth	Location of Birth	Date of Marriage	Location of Marriage	Date of Death	Location of Death

NOTES

Name	Date of Birth	Location of Birth	Date of Marriage	Location of Marriage	Date of Death	Location of Death

NOTES

_____

_____

_____

Name	Date of Birth	Location of Birth	Date of Marriage	Location of Marriage	Date of Death	Location of Death

NOTES

Name	Date of Birth	Location of Birth	Date of Marriage	Location of Marriage	Date of Death	Location of Death

NOTES

Name	Date of Birth	Location of Birth	Date of Marriage	Location of Marriage	Date of Death	Location of Death

NOTES

MOTHER SIDE FAMILY

Thank You
DAD
FOR
Everything

SUPER DAD

FATHER SIDE FAMILY

No.1 Mom

Mom

MOTHER SIDE FAMILY

Thank You
DAD
FOR
Everything

SUPER
DAD

FATHER SIDE FAMILY

No.1 Mom

Mom

MOTHER SIDE FAMILY

Thank You
DAD
FOR
Everything

SUPER
DAD

FATHER SIDE FAMILY

No.1 Mom

Mom

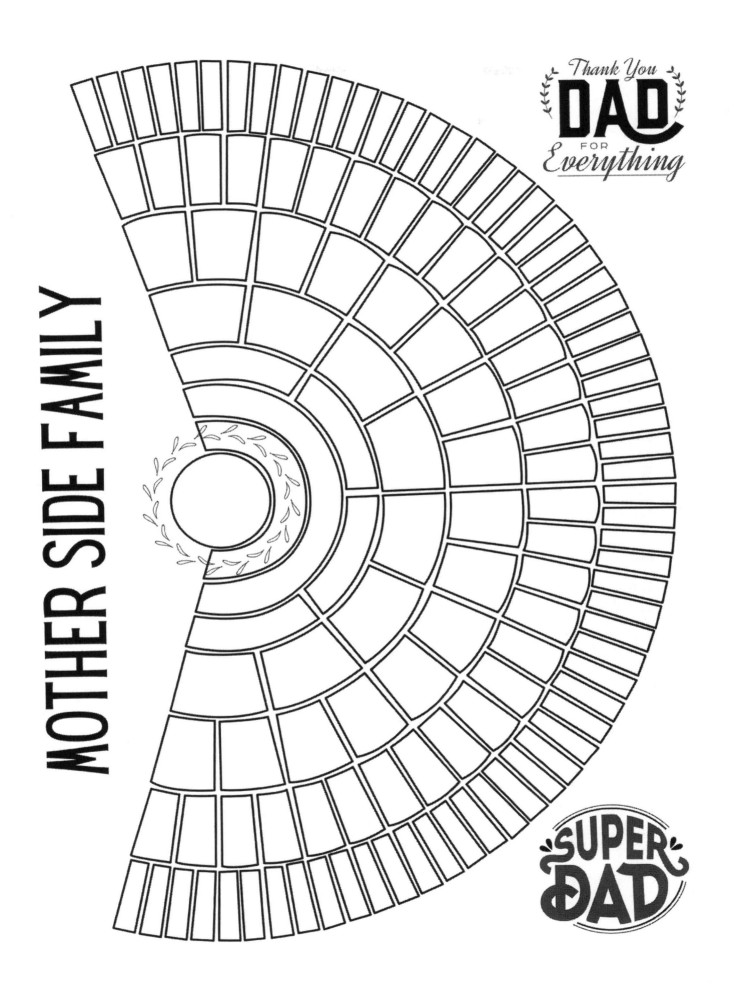

MOTHER SIDE FAMILY

Thank You
DAD
FOR
Everything

SUPER DAD

FATHER SIDE FAMILY

No.1 Mom

Mom

MOTHER SIDE FAMILY

Thank You
DAD
FOR
Everything

SUPER
DAD

FATHER SIDE FAMILY

No.1 Mom

Mom

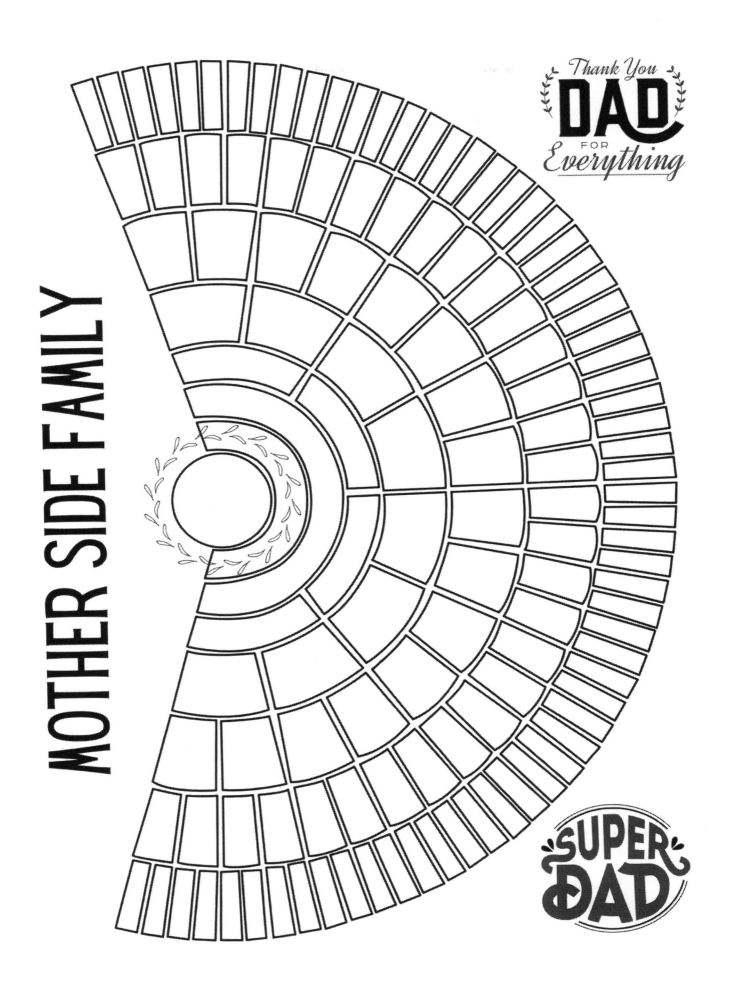

MOTHER SIDE FAMILY

Thank You DAD FOR Everything

SUPER DAD

FATHER SIDE FAMILY

No.1 Mom

Mom

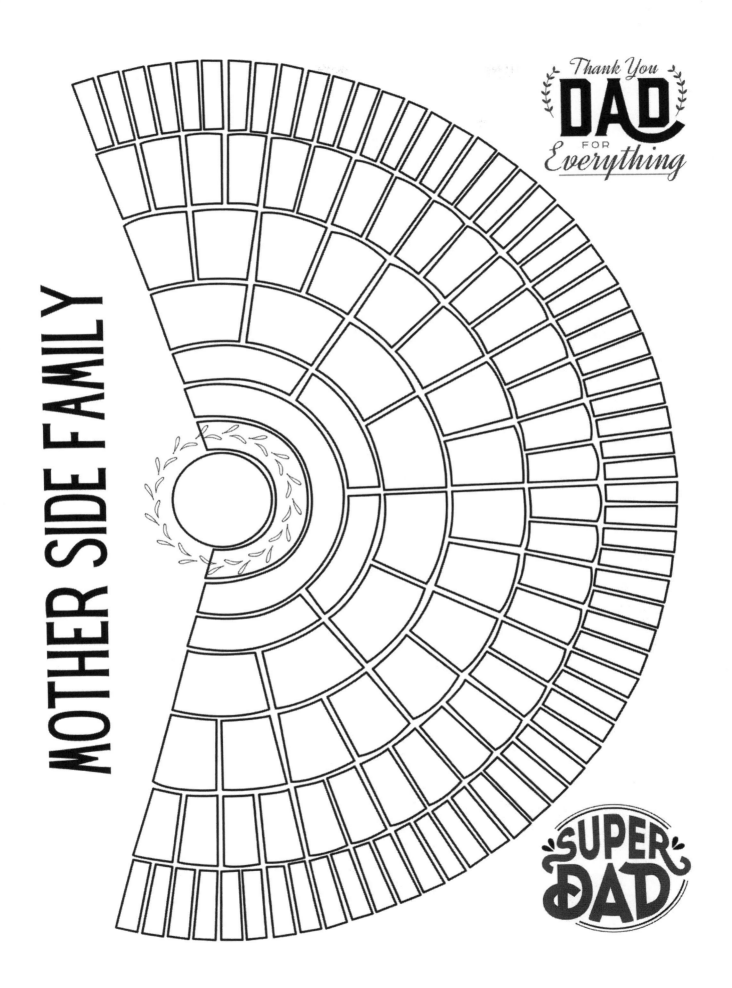

MOTHER SIDE FAMILY

Thank You DAD FOR Everything

SUPER DAD

FATHER SIDE FAMILY

No.1 Mom

Mom

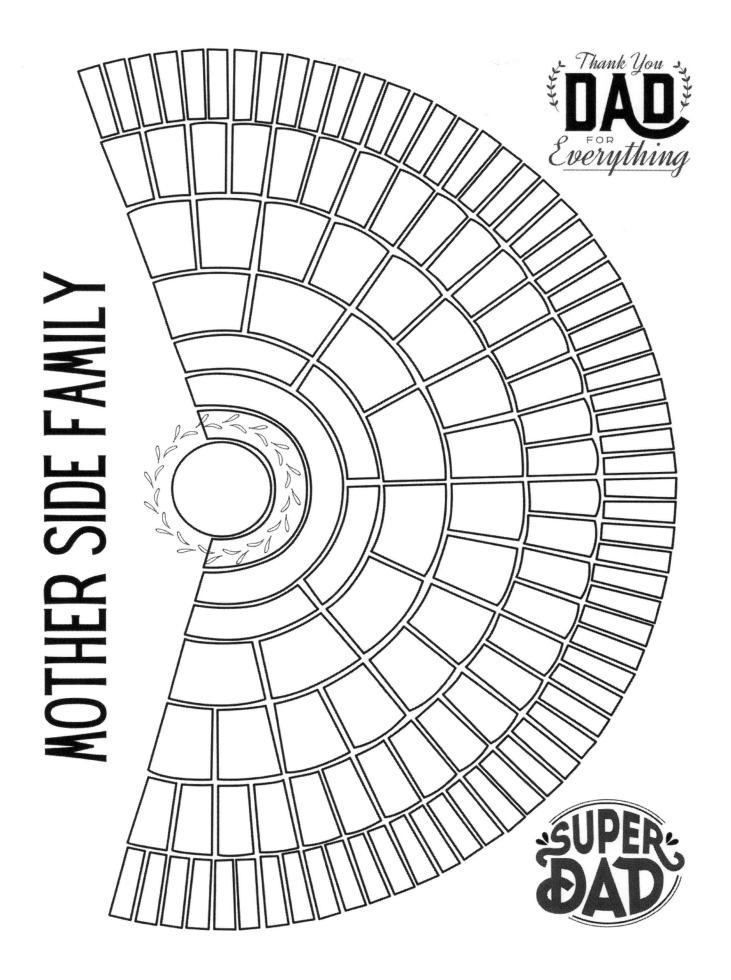

MOTHER SIDE FAMILY

Thank You
DAD
FOR
Everything

SUPER
DAD

FATHER SIDE FAMILY

No.1 Mom

Mom

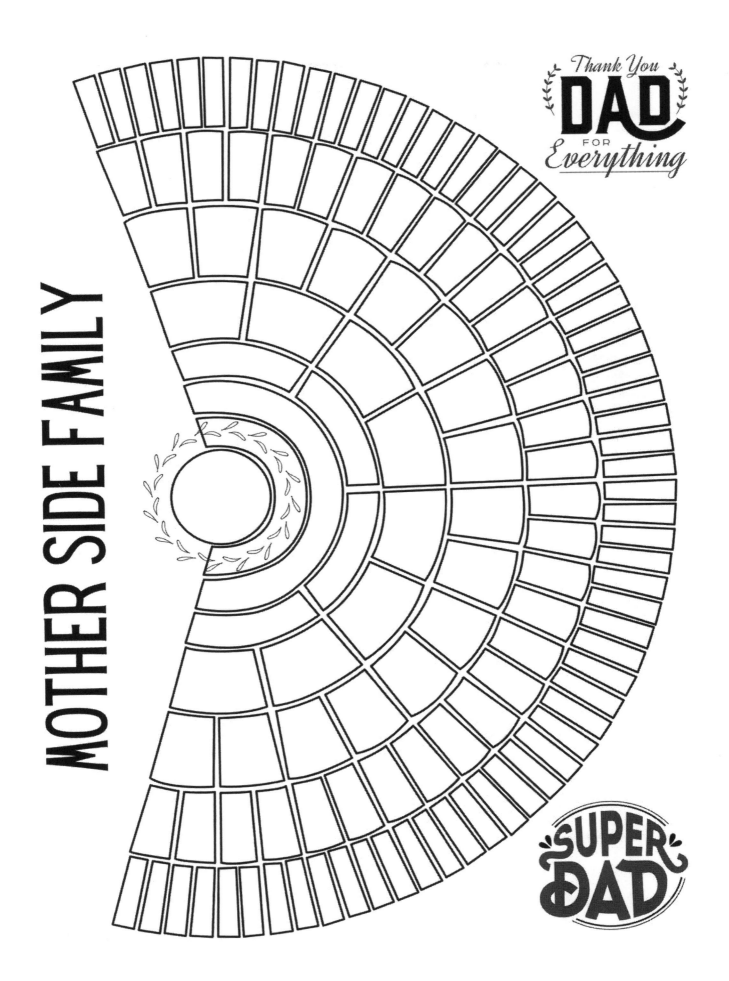

MOTHER SIDE FAMILY

Thank You
DAD
FOR
Everything

SUPER
DAD

FATHER SIDE FAMILY

No.1 Mom

Mom

MOTHER SIDE FAMILY

Thank You
DAD
FOR
Everything

SUPER
DAD

FATHER SIDE FAMILY

No.1 Mom

Mom

Name: _____

Place photo

Date of birth:
Date of death:
Burried location:

1

2

Name: _____
Father name: _____
Mother name: _____
Date of birth: _____
Burried location: _____
Date of death: _____

Name: _____
Father name: _____
Mother name: _____
Date of birth: _____
Burried location: _____
Date of death: _____

Name: _____
Father name: _____
Mother name: _____
Date of birth: _____
Burried location: _____
Date of death: _____

1

Name: _____
Father name: _____
Mother name: _____
Date of birth: _____
Burried location: _____
Date of death: _____

2

1

Name: _____
Father name: _____
Mother name: _____
Date of birth: _____
Burried location: _____
Date of death: _____

3

2

Name: _____
Father name: _____
Mother name: _____
Date of birth: _____
Burried location: _____
Date of death: _____

Name: _____

Place photo	Date of birth: Date of death: Burried location:

1

Name: _____
Father name: _____
Mother name: _____
Date of birth: _____
Burried location: _____
Date of death: _____

2

Name: _____
Father name: _____
Mother name: _____
Date of birth: _____
Burried location: _____
Date of death: _____

Name: _____
Father name: _____
Mother name: _____
Date of birth: _____
Burried location: _____
Date of death: _____

1

Name: _____
Father name: _____
Mother name: _____
Date of birth: _____
Burried location: _____
Date of death: _____

2

1

Name: _____
Father name: _____
Mother name: _____
Date of birth: _____
Burried location: _____
Date of death: _____

Name: _____
Father name: _____
Mother name: _____
Date of birth: _____
Burried location: _____
Date of death: _____

3

2

Name: _____
Father name: _____
Mother name: _____
Date of birth: _____
Burried location: _____
Date of death: _____

Name: _____

Place photo

Date of birth:
Date of death:
Burried location:

1

2

Name: _____
Father name: _____
Mother name: _____
Date of birth: _____
Burried location: _____
Date of death: _____

Name: _____
Father name: _____
Mother name: _____
Date of birth: _____
Burried location: _____
Date of death: _____

Name: _____
Father name: _____
Mother name: _____
Date of birth: _____
Burried location: _____
Date of death: _____

1

Name: _____
Father name: _____
Mother name: _____
Date of birth: _____
Burried location: _____
Date of death: _____

2

1

Name: _____
Father name: _____
Mother name: _____
Date of birth: _____
Burried location: _____
Date of death: _____

Name: _____
Father name: _____
Mother name: _____
Date of birth: _____
Burried location: _____
Date of death: _____

3

2

Name: _____
Father name: _____
Mother name: _____
Date of birth: _____
Burried location: _____
Date of death: _____

Name: _____

[Place photo]

Date of birth:
Date of death:
Burried location:

1

2

Name: _____
Father name: _____
Mother name: _____
Date of birth: _____
Burried location: _____
Date of death: _____

Name: _____
Father name: _____
Mother name: _____
Date of birth: _____
Burried location: _____
Date of death: _____

Name: _____
Father name: _____
Mother name: _____
Date of birth: _____
Burried location: _____
Date of death: _____

1

Name: _____
Father name: _____
Mother name: _____
Date of birth: _____
Burried location: _____
Date of death: _____

2

1

Name: _____
Father name: _____
Mother name: _____
Date of birth: _____
Burried location: _____
Date of death: _____

Name: _____
Father name: _____
Mother name: _____
Date of birth: _____
Burried location: _____
Date of death: _____

3

2

Name: _____
Father name: _____
Mother name: _____
Date of birth: _____
Burried location: _____
Date of death: _____

Name: _____

Place photo

Date of birth:
Date of death:
Burried location:

1

Name: _____
Father name: _____
Mother name: _____
Date of birth: _____
Burried location: _____
Date of death: _____

2

Name: _____
Father name: _____
Mother name: _____
Date of birth: _____
Burried location: _____
Date of death: _____

Name: _____
Father name: _____
Mother name: _____
Date of birth: _____
Burried location: _____
Date of death: _____

1

Name: _____
Father name: _____
Mother name: _____
Date of birth: _____
Burried location: _____
Date of death: _____

2

1

Name: _____
Father name: _____
Mother name: _____
Date of birth: _____
Burried location: _____
Date of death: _____

Name: _____
Father name: _____
Mother name: _____
Date of birth: _____
Burried location: _____
Date of death: _____

3

2

Name: _____
Father name: _____
Mother name: _____
Date of birth: _____
Burried location: _____
Date of death: _____

Name: _____

Place photo

Date of birth:
Date of death:
Burried location:

1

2

1

Name: _____
Father name: _____
Mother name: _____
Date of birth: _____
Burried location: _____
Date of death: _____

2

Name: _____
Father name: _____
Mother name: _____
Date of birth: _____
Burried location: _____
Date of death: _____

1

Name: _____
Father name: _____
Mother name: _____
Date of birth: _____
Burried location: _____
Date of death: _____

2

Name: _____
Father name: _____
Mother name: _____
Date of birth: _____
Burried location: _____
Date of death: _____

3

Name: _____
Father name: _____
Mother name: _____
Date of birth: _____
Burried location: _____
Date of death: _____

1

Name: _____
Father name: _____
Mother name: _____
Date of birth: _____
Burried location: _____
Date of death: _____

2

Name: _____
Father name: _____
Mother name: _____
Date of birth: _____
Burried location: _____
Date of death: _____

Name: _____

Place photo	**Date of birth:** **Date of death:** **Burried location:**

1

2

Name: _____
Father name: _____
Mother name: _____
Date of birth: _____
Burried location: _____
Date of death: _____

Name: _____
Father name: _____
Mother name: _____
Date of birth: _____
Burried location: _____
Date of death: _____

1

Name: _____
Father name: _____
Mother name: _____
Date of birth: _____
Burried location: _____
Date of death: _____

2

Name: _____
Father name: _____
Mother name: _____
Date of birth: _____
Burried location: _____
Date of death: _____

1

Name: _____
Father name: _____
Mother name: _____
Date of birth: _____
Burried location: _____
Date of death: _____

2

Name: _____
Father name: _____
Mother name: _____
Date of birth: _____
Burried location: _____
Date of death: _____

3

Name: _____
Father name: _____
Mother name: _____
Date of birth: _____
Burried location: _____
Date of death: _____

Name: _____

Place photo

Date of birth:
Date of death:
Burried location:

1

2

Name: _____
Father name: _____
Mother name: _____
Date of birth: _____
Burried location: _____
Date of death: _____

Name: _____
Father name: _____
Mother name: _____
Date of birth: _____
Burried location: _____
Date of death: _____

Name: _____
Father name: _____
Mother name: _____
Date of birth: _____
Burried location: _____
Date of death: _____

1

Name: _____
Father name: _____
Mother name: _____
Date of birth: _____
Burried location: _____
Date of death: _____

2

1

Name: _____
Father name: _____
Mother name: _____
Date of birth: _____
Burried location: _____
Date of death: _____

Name: _____
Father name: _____
Mother name: _____
Date of birth: _____
Burried location: _____
Date of death: _____

3

2

Name: _____
Father name: _____
Mother name: _____
Date of birth: _____
Burried location: _____
Date of death: _____

Name: _____

Place photo

Date of birth:
Date of death:
Burried location:

1

2

Name: _____
Father name: _____
Mother name: _____
Date of birth: _____
Burried location: _____
Date of death: _____

Name: _____
Father name: _____
Mother name: _____
Date of birth: _____
Burried location: _____
Date of death: _____

Name: _____
Father name: _____
Mother name: _____
Date of birth: _____
Burried location: _____
Date of death: _____

1

Name: _____
Father name: _____
Mother name: _____
Date of birth: _____
Burried location: _____
Date of death: _____

2

1

Name: _____
Father name: _____
Mother name: _____
Date of birth: _____
Burried location: _____
Date of death: _____

Name: _____
Father name: _____
Mother name: _____
Date of birth: _____
Burried location: _____
Date of death: _____

3

2

Name: _____
Father name: _____
Mother name: _____
Date of birth: _____
Burried location: _____
Date of death: _____

Name: _____

Place photo

Date of birth:
Date of death:
Burried location:

1

Name: _____
Father name: _____
Mother name: _____
Date of birth: _____
Burried location: _____
Date of death: _____

2

Name: _____
Father name: _____
Mother name: _____
Date of birth: _____
Burried location: _____
Date of death: _____

Name: _____
Father name: _____
Mother name: _____
Date of birth: _____
Burried location: _____
Date of death: _____

1

Name: _____
Father name: _____
Mother name: _____
Date of birth: _____
Burried location: _____
Date of death: _____

2

1

Name: _____
Father name: _____
Mother name: _____
Date of birth: _____
Burried location: _____
Date of death: _____

Name: _____
Father name: _____
Mother name: _____
Date of birth: _____
Burried location: _____
Date of death: _____

3

2

Name: _____
Father name: _____
Mother name: _____
Date of birth: _____
Burried location: _____
Date of death: _____

Name: _____

Place photo

Date of birth:
Date of death:
Burried location:

1

2

Name: _____
Father name: _____
Mother name: _____
Date of birth: _____
Burried location: _____
Date of death: _____

Name: _____
Father name: _____
Mother name: _____
Date of birth: _____
Burried location: _____
Date of death: _____

Name: _____
Father name: _____
Mother name: _____
Date of birth: _____
Burried location: _____
Date of death: _____

1

Name: _____
Father name: _____
Mother name: _____
Date of birth: _____
Burried location: _____
Date of death: _____

2

1

Name: _____
Father name: _____
Mother name: _____
Date of birth: _____
Burried location: _____
Date of death: _____

Name: _____
Father name: _____
Mother name: _____
Date of birth: _____
Burried location: _____
Date of death: _____

3

2

Name: _____
Father name: _____
Mother name: _____
Date of birth: _____
Burried location: _____
Date of death: _____

Name: _____

Place photo

Date of birth:
Date of death:
Burried location:

1

Name: _____
Father name: _____
Mother name: _____
Date of birth: _____
Burried location: _____
Date of death: _____

2

Name: _____
Father name: _____
Mother name: _____
Date of birth: _____
Burried location: _____
Date of death: _____

Name: _____
Father name: _____
Mother name: _____
Date of birth: _____
Burried location: _____
Date of death: _____

1

Name: _____
Father name: _____
Mother name: _____
Date of birth: _____
Burried location: _____
Date of death: _____

2

1

Name: _____
Father name: _____
Mother name: _____
Date of birth: _____
Burried location: _____
Date of death: _____

Name: _____
Father name: _____
Mother name: _____
Date of birth: _____
Burried location: _____
Date of death: _____

3

2

Name: _____
Father name: _____
Mother name: _____
Date of birth: _____
Burried location: _____
Date of death: _____

Name: _____

[Place photo]

Date of birth:
Date of death:
Burried location:

1

2

Name: _____
Father name: _____
Mother name: _____
Date of birth: _____
Burried location: _____
Date of death: _____

Name: _____
Father name: _____
Mother name: _____
Date of birth: _____
Burried location: _____
Date of death: _____

Name: _____
Father name: _____
Mother name: _____
Date of birth: _____
Burried location: _____
Date of death: _____

1

Name: _____
Father name: _____
Mother name: _____
Date of birth: _____
Burried location: _____
Date of death: _____

2

1

Name: _____
Father name: _____
Mother name: _____
Date of birth: _____
Burried location: _____
Date of death: _____

Name: _____
Father name: _____
Mother name: _____
Date of birth: _____
Burried location: _____
Date of death: _____

3

2

Name: _____
Father name: _____
Mother name: _____
Date of birth: _____
Burried location: _____
Date of death: _____

Name: _____

Place photo

Date of birth:
Date of death:
Burried location:

1

Name: _____
Father name: _____
Mother name: _____
Date of birth: _____
Burried location: _____
Date of death: _____

2

Name: _____
Father name: _____
Mother name: _____
Date of birth: _____
Burried location: _____
Date of death: _____

1

Name: _____
Father name: _____
Mother name: _____
Date of birth: _____
Burried location: _____
Date of death: _____

2

Name: _____
Father name: _____
Mother name: _____
Date of birth: _____
Burried location: _____
Date of death: _____

3

Name: _____
Father name: _____
Mother name: _____
Date of birth: _____
Burried location: _____
Date of death: _____

1

Name: _____
Father name: _____
Mother name: _____
Date of birth: _____
Burried location: _____
Date of death: _____

2

Name: _____
Father name: _____
Mother name: _____
Date of birth: _____
Burried location: _____
Date of death: _____

Name: _____

Place photo

Date of birth:
Date of death:
Burried location:

1

2

Name: _____
Father name: _____
Mother name: _____
Date of birth: _____
Burried location: _____
Date of death: _____

Name: _____
Father name: _____
Mother name: _____
Date of birth: _____
Burried location: _____
Date of death: _____

Name: _____
Father name: _____
Mother name: _____
Date of birth: _____
Burried location: _____
Date of death: _____

1

Name: _____
Father name: _____
Mother name: _____
Date of birth: _____
Burried location: _____
Date of death: _____

1

Name: _____
Father name: _____
Mother name: _____
Date of birth: _____
Burried location: _____
Date of death: _____

2

Name: _____
Father name: _____
Mother name: _____
Date of birth: _____
Burried location: _____
Date of death: _____

2

Name: _____
Father name: _____
Mother name: _____
Date of birth: _____
Burried location: _____
Date of death: _____

3

Name: _____

Place photo

Date of birth:
Date of death:
Burried location:

1

Name: _____
Father name: _____
Mother name: _____
Date of birth: _____
Burried location: _____
Date of death: _____

2

Name: _____
Father name: _____
Mother name: _____
Date of birth: _____
Burried location: _____
Date of death: _____

1

Name: _____
Father name: _____
Mother name: _____
Date of birth: _____
Burried location: _____
Date of death: _____

2

Name: _____
Father name: _____
Mother name: _____
Date of birth: _____
Burried location: _____
Date of death: _____

1

Name: _____
Father name: _____
Mother name: _____
Date of birth: _____
Burried location: _____
Date of death: _____

3

Name: _____
Father name: _____
Mother name: _____
Date of birth: _____
Burried location: _____
Date of death: _____

2

Name: _____
Father name: _____
Mother name: _____
Date of birth: _____
Burried location: _____
Date of death: _____

Name: _____

Place photo

Date of birth:
Date of death:
Burried location:

1

2

Name: _____
Father name: _____
Mother name: _____
Date of birth: _____
Burried location: _____
Date of death: _____

Name: _____
Father name: _____
Mother name: _____
Date of birth: _____
Burried location: _____
Date of death: _____

Name: _____
Father name: _____
Mother name: _____
Date of birth: _____
Burried location: _____
Date of death: _____

1

Name: _____
Father name: _____
Mother name: _____
Date of birth: _____
Burried location: _____
Date of death: _____

2

1

Name: _____
Father name: _____
Mother name: _____
Date of birth: _____
Burried location: _____
Date of death: _____

Name: _____
Father name: _____
Mother name: _____
Date of birth: _____
Burried location: _____
Date of death: _____

3

2

Name: _____
Father name: _____
Mother name: _____
Date of birth: _____
Burried location: _____
Date of death: _____

Name: _____

[Place photo]

Date of birth:
Date of death:
Burried location:

1

Name: _____
Father name: _____
Mother name: _____
Date of birth: _____
Burried location: _____
Date of death: _____

2

Name: _____
Father name: _____
Mother name: _____
Date of birth: _____
Burried location: _____
Date of death: _____

Name: _____
Father name: _____
Mother name: _____
Date of birth: _____
Burried location: _____
Date of death: _____

1

Name: _____
Father name: _____
Mother name: _____
Date of birth: _____
Burried location: _____
Date of death: _____

2

1

Name: _____
Father name: _____
Mother name: _____
Date of birth: _____
Burried location: _____
Date of death: _____

Name: _____
Father name: _____
Mother name: _____
Date of birth: _____
Burried location: _____
Date of death: _____

3

2

Name: _____
Father name: _____
Mother name: _____
Date of birth: _____
Burried location: _____
Date of death: _____

Name: _____

Place photo

Date of birth:
Date of death:
Burried location:

1

2

Name: _____
Father name: _____
Mother name: _____
Date of birth: _____
Burried location: _____
Date of death: _____

Name: _____
Father name: _____
Mother name: _____
Date of birth: _____
Burried location: _____
Date of death: _____

Name: _____
Father name: _____
Mother name: _____
Date of birth: _____
Burried location: _____
Date of death: _____

1

Name: _____
Father name: _____
Mother name: _____
Date of birth: _____
Burried location: _____
Date of death: _____

2

1

Name: _____
Father name: _____
Mother name: _____
Date of birth: _____
Burried location: _____
Date of death: _____

Name: _____
Father name: _____
Mother name: _____
Date of birth: _____
Burried location: _____
Date of death: _____

3

2

Name: _____
Father name: _____
Mother name: _____
Date of birth: _____
Burried location: _____
Date of death: _____

Name: _____

Place photo

Date of birth:
Date of death:
Burried location:

1 **2**

Name: _____
Father name: _____
Mother name: _____
Date of birth: _____
Burried location: _____
Date of death: _____

Name: _____
Father name: _____
Mother name: _____
Date of birth: _____
Burried location: _____
Date of death: _____

Name: _____
Father name: _____
Mother name: _____
Date of birth: _____
Burried location: _____
Date of death: _____

1

Name: _____
Father name: _____
Mother name: _____
Date of birth: _____
Burried location: _____
Date of death: _____

2

1

Name: _____
Father name: _____
Mother name: _____
Date of birth: _____
Burried location: _____
Date of death: _____

Name: _____
Father name: _____
Mother name: _____
Date of birth: _____
Burried location: _____
Date of death: _____

3

2

Name: _____
Father name: _____
Mother name: _____
Date of birth: _____
Burried location: _____
Date of death: _____

Genealogy Organizer

Name:

Date Of Birth:

Date Of Death:

Location Of Birth:

Location Of Death:

Mother:

Father:

Spouses	Children

Genealogy Organizer

Name:

Date Of Birth:

Date Of Death:

Location Of Birth:

Location Of Death:

Mother:

Father:

Spouses

Children

Genealogy Organizer

Name:

Date Of Birth:

Date Of Death:

Location Of Birth:

Location Of Death:

Mother:

Father:

Spouses	Children

Genealogy Organizer

Name:

Date Of Birth:

Date Of Death:

Location Of Birth:

Location Of Death:

Mother:

Father:

Spouses

Children

Genealogy Organizer

Name:

Date Of Birth:

Date Of Death:

Location Of Birth:

Location Of Death:

Mother:

Father:

Spouses	Children

Genealogy Organizer

Name:

Date Of Birth:

Date Of Death:

Location Of Birth:

Location Of Death:

Mother:

Father:

Spouses

Children

Genealogy Organizer

Name:

Date Of Birth:

Date Of Death:

Location Of Birth:

Location Of Death:

Mother:

Father:

Spouses	Children

Genealogy Organizer

Name:

Date Of Birth:

Date Of Death:

Location Of Birth:

Location Of Death:

Mother:

Father:

Spouses

Children

Genealogy Organizer

Name:

Date Of Birth:

Date Of Death:

Location Of Birth:

Location Of Death:

Mother:

Father:

Spouses	Children

Genealogy Organizer

Name:

Date Of Birth:

Date Of Death:

Location Of Birth:

Location Of Death:

Mother:

Father:

Spouses	Children

Genealogy Organizer

Name:

Date Of Birth:

Date Of Death:

Location Of Birth:

Location Of Death:

Mother:

Father:

Spouses	Children

Genealogy Organizer

Name:

Date Of Birth:

Date Of Death:

Location Of Birth:

Location Of Death:

Mother:

Father:

Spouses

Children

Genealogy Organizer

Name:

Date Of Birth:

Date Of Death:

Location Of Birth:

Location Of Death:

Mother:

Father:

Spouses

Children

Genealogy Organizer

Name:

Date Of Birth:

Date Of Death:

Location Of Birth:

Location Of Death:

Mother:

Father:

Spouses	Children

Genealogy Organizer

Name:

Date Of Birth:

Date Of Death:

Location Of Birth:

Location Of Death:

Mother:

Father:

Spouses

Children

Genealogy Organizer

Name:

Date Of Birth:

Date Of Death:

Location Of Birth:

Location Of Death:

Mother:

Father:

Spouses	Children

Genealogy Organizer

Name:

Date Of Birth:

Date Of Death:

Location Of Birth:

Location Of Death:

Mother:

Father:

Spouses

Children

Genealogy Organizer

Name:

Date Of Birth:

Date Of Death:

Location Of Birth:

Location Of Death:

Mother:

Father:

Spouses	Children

Genealogy Organizer

Name:

Date Of Birth:

Date Of Death:

Location Of Birth:

Location Of Death:

Mother:

Father:

Spouses	Children

Genealogy Organizer

Name:

Date Of Birth:

Date Of Death:

Location Of Birth:

Location Of Death:

Mother:

Father:

Spouses	Children

Genealogy Organizer Notebook

Name:	**Name:**
Born:	**Born:**
Died:	**Died:**

Children:

Name:		**Name:**	
Born:		**Born:**	
Place:		**Place:**	
Died:		**Died:**	
Place:		**Place:**	
Spouse:		**Spouse:**	
Notes:		**Notes:**	
Name:		**Name:**	
Born:		**Born:**	
Place:		**Place:**	
Died:		**Died:**	
Place:		**Place:**	
Spouse:		**Spouse:**	
Notes:		**Notes:**	
Name:		**Name:**	
Born:		**Born:**	
Place:		**Place:**	
Died:		**Died:**	

Genealogy Organizer Notebook

Name:		Name:	
Born:		Born:	
Died:		Died:	

Children:	

Name:		Name:	
Born:		Born:	
Place:		Place:	
Died:		Died:	
Place:		Place:	
Spouse:		Spouse:	
Notes:		Notes:	
Name:		Name:	
Born:		Born:	
Place:		Place:	
Died:		Died:	
Place:		Place:	
Spouse:		Spouse:	
Notes:		Notes:	
Name:		Name:	
Born:		Born:	
Place:		Place:	
Died:		Died:	

Genealogy Organizer Notebook

Name:	Name:
Born:	Born:
Died:	Died:

Children:

Name:		Name:	
Born:		Born:	
Place:		Place:	
Died:		Died:	
Place:		Place:	
Spouse:		Spouse:	
Notes:		Notes:	
Name:		Name:	
Born:		Born:	
Place:		Place:	
Died:		Died:	
Place:		Place:	
Spouse:		Spouse:	
Notes:		Notes:	
Name:		Name:	
Born:		Born:	
Place:		Place:	
Died:		Died:	

Genealogy Organizer Notebook

Name:		Name:
Born:		Born:
Died:		Died:

Children:

Name:		Name:	
Born:		Born:	
Place:		Place:	
Died:		Died:	
Place:		Place:	
Spouse:		Spouse:	
Notes:		Notes:	

Name:		Name:	
Born:		Born:	
Place:		Place:	
Died:		Died:	
Place:		Place:	
Spouse:		Spouse:	
Notes:		Notes:	

Name:		Name:	
Born:		Born:	
Place:		Place:	
Died:		Died:	

Genealogy Organizer Notebook

Name:	**Name:**
Born:	**Born:**
Died:	**Died:**

Children:

Name:		**Name:**	
Born:		**Born:**	
Place:		**Place:**	
Died:		**Died:**	
Place:		**Place:**	
Spouse:		**Spouse:**	
Notes:		**Notes:**	

Name:		**Name:**	
Born:		**Born:**	
Place:		**Place:**	
Died:		**Died:**	
Place:		**Place:**	
Spouse:		**Spouse:**	
Notes:		**Notes:**	

Name:		**Name:**	
Born:		**Born:**	
Place:		**Place:**	
Died:		**Died:**	

Genealogy Organizer Notebook

Name:	Name:
Born:	Born:
Died:	Died:

Children:

Name:		Name:	
Born:		Born:	
Place:		Place:	
Died:		Died:	
Place:		Place:	
Spouse:		Spouse:	
Notes:		Notes:	
Name:		Name:	
Born:		Born:	
Place:		Place:	
Died:		Died:	
Place:		Place:	
Spouse:		Spouse:	
Notes:		Notes:	
Name:		Name:	
Born:		Born:	
Place:		Place:	
Died:		Died:	

Genealogy Organizer Notebook

Name:	Name:
Born:	Born:
Died:	Died:

Children:	

Name:		Name:	
Born:		Born:	
Place:		Place:	
Died:		Died:	
Place:		Place:	
Spouse:		Spouse:	
Notes:		Notes:	
Name:		Name:	
Born:		Born:	
Place:		Place:	
Died:		Died:	
Place:		Place:	
Spouse:		Spouse:	
Notes:		Notes:	
Name:		Name:	
Born:		Born:	
Place:		Place:	
Died:		Died:	

Genealogy Organizer Notebook

Name:	Name:
Born:	Born:
Died:	Died:

Children:	

Name:		Name:	
Born:		Born:	
Place:		Place:	
Died:		Died:	
Place:		Place:	
Spouse:		Spouse:	
Notes:		Notes:	
Name:		Name:	
Born:		Born:	
Place:		Place:	
Died:		Died:	
Place:		Place:	
Spouse:		Spouse:	
Notes:		Notes:	
Name:		Name:	
Born:		Born:	
Place:		Place:	
Died:		Died:	

Genealogy Organizer Notebook

Name:

Born:

Died:

Name:

Born:

Died:

Children:

Name:

Born:

Place:

Died:

Place:

Spouse:

Notes:

Name:

Born:

Place:

Died:

Place:

Spouse:

Notes:

Name:

Born:

Place:

Died:

Name:

Born:

Place:

Died:

Place:

Spouse:

Notes:

Name:

Born:

Place:

Died:

Place:

Spouse:

Notes:

Name:

Born:

Place:

Died:

Genealogy Organizer Notebook

Name:	Name:
Born:	Born:
Died:	Died:

Children:	

Name:		Name:	
Born:		Born:	
Place:		Place:	
Died:		Died:	
Place:		Place:	
Spouse:		Spouse:	
Notes:		Notes:	
Name:		Name:	
Born:		Born:	
Place:		Place:	
Died:		Died:	
Place:		Place:	
Spouse:		Spouse:	
Notes:		Notes:	
Name:		Name:	
Born:		Born:	
Place:		Place:	
Died:		Died:	

Made in the USA
Las Vegas, NV
29 January 2025

17138841R00061